Houston in 3 Days:

The Definitive Tourist Guide Book That Helps You Travel Smart and Save Time

Finest City Guides

Book Description

Houston is the largest city in Texas, and it's a city that's calling your name if you're looking for unique cultural, entertainment, historical and culinary experiences. It offers museums, festivals, restaurants and other sights that celebrate worldwide cultures.

Houston in 3 Days is more than a generic itinerary for travelers. It will lead you to the best sights that everyone wants to see, but also to eclectic, out of the way places that you'll be so happy to have found.

Create your own history and experience in the fourth largest city in the United States. Whether you've been to Houston before, or are a first-time visitor, this book will lead you on a well-planned journey.

We'll show you:

- The best hotels in three price ranges
- The best food, from fine dining to cheap eats
- Sightseeing highlights
- Best neighborhoods to visit
- Shopping opportunities
- How to get around
- What kind of currency Texans use

Plan ahead and make this the best trip you've ever taken!

The People of Houston

Houston is an international, diverse city, with links to aerospace, manufacturing, energy and biomedical fields. The population as of 2014 was 2.24 million.

The demographics of Houston are unique, too. The population is nearly 50% white, which includes Latinos and Hispanics. Over 25% of the city is African American or black, and more than

5% are Asian. The city also includes Pacific Islanders, 16.5% people of other races and 3% who are two or more races.

The local paper, the Daily Mail, refers to the 2000 census, which shows that the ethnic and racial diversity in the Houston area has increased in areas that are outside of the downtown area, where the cost of living is lower and there is more residential development.

Everything is bigger in Texas – you may have heard that before. It's not precisely true, although the state is one of the largest, geographically. The hearts of the people are big, and maybe that's the most welcoming thing about Houston.

Language

Nearly 90 languages are spoken regularly in the greater Houston metropolitan area. Roughly one million people speak only English. The most often spoken foreign languages are Spanish and

Spanish creole. Residents also speak Vietnamese, Chinese, indigenous African languages and Urdu. Many of the people who speak other languages in the home also speak English.

Holidays

New Year's Day	January 1
Martin Luther King, Jr. Day	January
George Washington's Birthday	February
Memorial Day	May
Independence Day	July 4
Labor Day	September
Columbus Day	October
Veterans Day	November
Thanksgiving Day	November
Christmas Day	December 25

Religious Beliefs

The Pew Research Center determined in a 2014 study that 73% of Houston identified themselves as Christian. 50% of these said they attended Protestant churches, and 19% Roman Catholic. 20% of the population don't claim a religious affiliation. Roughly 7% of people in Houston practice one of Hinduism, Islam, Buddhism or Judaism.

Here is a quick preview of what you will learn in this tourist guide:

- Helpful information about Houston
- Flying into the city
- Transportation tips in town
- Why Houston is such a vibrant tourist spot and what you will find most remarkable about it
- Information on luxury and budget accommodations and what you'll get for your money
- The currency used in Houston
- Tourist attractions you should make time to see
- Other attractions for entertainment and culture
- Events that may be running during your stay
- Tips on the best places to eat & drink for all price points, whether you want simple fare, worldwide dishes or Tex-Mex flavor

Table of Contents

Introduction 1
1. Key Information about Houston 9
2. Transport to and in Houston 12
3. Accommodations 16
4. Sightseeing 22
5. Eat & Drink 25
6. Culture and Entertainment 31
7. Special Events in Houston 36
8. Safety in Houston 44
Conclusion 46

Introduction

If you stop to think about Houston, Texas, it probably brings to mind oil refineries, baseball and oppressive heat. There is much more to Houston than that, so don't dismiss it from your vacation plans.

Houston is the number one creator of jobs of all American cities. More than 25 Fortune 500 companies make their home there. The cost of living is so low that your dollar goes farther than it would anywhere else in the US. It also has a thriving cultural and restaurant scene.

A Brief History of Houston
Houston began in August of 1836, when two men ran an ad in the local Telegraph & Texas Register for the "Town of Houston". The land of the to-be town included grassland and timber, and it was on a level coastal plain.

Houston in the 19th century was a political boomtown, but its very livelihood was dependent on commerce and cotton. The government moved to Austin from Houston, so the city settled into an agricultural rhythm. Many businessmen established new trade connections.

In 1856, a railway joined Houston with the Colorado Railway. In 1861, Houston had become the railway center of the southeast part of Texas, with five lines that stretched from 50-100 miles in all directions.

Construction of buildings and roads was interrupted by the Civil War, but was revived soon afterward. The railroads eventually spanned the coastal prairie bogs. Even while there were roads even from the beginning of the town, traveling was slow, and often rough.

Improved roads, transportation systems and systems necessary for telephone, telegraph and mail delivery helped Houston develop as a lumber and cotton market in the 19th century.

Oil was discovered near Houston and changed the city going into the 20th century. Refineries were erected along the inland Houston Ship Channel, safe from the storms in the Gulf of Mexico. By 1930, there were 40 oil companies with offices in Houston.

World War II created an increased demand for gasoline, synthetic rubber, ships and materials for explosives from the Houston area. Mid-size warships, concrete barges and steel merchant vessels were all built in areas along the Houston Ship Channel.

After WW II, the main exports of Houston were still related to petroleum. New fields of discovery would come to Houston in the 1960's, when the United States' National Aeronautics and Space Administration (NASA) choose Houston as its location for the new Manned Spacecraft Center. It opened in 1963. In fact, in 1969, the first word that was spoken on the moon was "Houston", during the mission of Apollo 11.

Houston became a capital of world energy in the 1970s. With rises in oil prices, due to an Arab oil embargo, the demand was higher for Texas oil and the city expanded. But it suffered with the oil downturn in the 1980s. The population of Houston declined during the 80s, for the only time ever.

In the 2000's, Houston welcomed over 125,000 residents of Gulf states displaced by Hurricane Katrina, one of the most serious hurricanes on record in the United States. The Astrodome was used for shelter and food. Houston has proven itself to be a giving city, as well as an urban metropolis.

Neighborhoods
When you look down on Houston from your plane as you arrive, it appears as though they have two downtown areas, both boasting high-rises. It wasn't intended, but Houston does not have any zoning, so you can build anything, anywhere. There are still a few distinct neighborhoods, though.

Neighborhoods Located Inside the Loop

Midtown

This is among the trendiest neighborhoods in Houston, sitting between the Museum District and the downtown area. Those living in lofts here share views of old oaks to the south and the skyline of downtown to the north. In addition to being home to young professionals, it offers wonderful food choices. There are also impressive galleries, contemporary crafts and theater.

Downtown

The downtown area is evolving as an entertainment, business and theater district. It has four pro sports team and a massive selection of nightclubs and restaurants. Houston was ranked as being the 6th best Restaurant City found in the US, according to Forbes Traveler. Main street is a nightlife hub, with over 70 clubs and bars from which to make a choice.

Montrose

This is an area of diversity and eccentricity, where you can find museums, art galleries, antique stores and fine restaurants. There are also vintage clothing boutiques, tattoo parlors and tarot readers. Sidewalk cafes, coffeehouses, a variety of architecture and large gay and Hispanic populations also add to the style and variety.

Neighborhoods Found Outside the Loop

Southwest

This neighborhood is made up of unique, smaller areas that reflect the city's diversity. It is home to educational, shopping and entertainment venues. Houston's Chinatown is the second largest community of Indochinese residents, after Los Angeles, in the US.

Uptown

Uptown has shady oaks, lush plantings and trademark steel arches, the Uptown district is a great place for Houston shoppers. It offers shopping spread over five million square feet, which includes The Galleria, which is the fourth largest center for shopping in the United States.

Neighborhoods Located Outside the Beltway

Memorial Area

This multi-neighborhood, suburban area straddles the outer loop, just went from downtown Houston. There is plenty of shopping and a ton of restaurants.

Bay Area

This is Houston's waterfront paradise. It actually includes seven separate cities! It has over 35 miles located on the waterfront. It is the home of the space programs of Mission Control, while it also offers nature preserves, exceptional shopping and succulent seafood.

What does Houston offer its Visitors?

It's easy to find fun in Houston. Their downtown area is revitalized, with musical entertainment, numerous clubs and professional sports facilities, that all brought the nightlife back to Houston's downtown. The city also offers many attractions, and restaurants and shopping that fit any budget.

1. Key Information about Houston

Money Matters

Houston, like all cities in the US, uses the US dollar (USD). The most commonly used bills include 100, 50, 20, 10, 5 and 1.

100 cents are equal to $1, and the coins you'll see include 50 (rarely), 25, 10, 5 and 1 cent.

Banks and ATMs

If you travel on credit or debit cards, there are plenty of banks and ATMs in Houston.

If you're visiting from abroad, you can save fees by using your credit card. Other than street vendors, they are accepted almost anywhere, and you can even charge purchases lower than $1.

When you pay by credit card, they use the current exchange rate, and the high max fee is usually only about one percent.

Exchanging Money

If you'd rather pay with cash, you can exchange foreign currency for American money at a currency exchange house or a local bank. Be sure to check to see the fees that your bank will charge for foreign cash withdrawals.

Tipping

Like all US destinations, tipping is encouraged and even expected. You may pay your doorman at the hotel $1-$2 if he hails a cab for you. If he is carrying your bags, the generally acceptable tip is $2 for your first bag and then $1 for any additional bags. They don't need to be tipped if all they do is open the door. Bellhops are usually tipped the same as doormen.

For maid service, most travelers leave $3 - $5 per day. The maids change daily, so you can leave your tip on the pillow to make sure they get it.

If your hotel front desk staff makes reservations for you or helps you plan an excursion, slip him or her $5 or so, too.

Restaurant Tipping

In full service restaurants, where you are waited on at your table, tipping is customarily 15-20%, rounded to the nearest dollar. If you happen to use a coupon, the tips are calculated on the full amount, not the discounted cost.

2. Transport to and in Houston

Getting to Houston by Plane

Houston is served mainly by George Bush Intercontinental Airport, when it comes to international flights. It's just 23 miles from the downtown area. Named after the United States' 41st president, not his son, the 43rd, it has many international and domestic flights. This massive airport served more than 43,000,000 passengers in 2015, which means it was the 10th busiest airport by passenger count in North America.

Getting to Houston from George Bush Intercontinental Airport

The Metro Transit Authority of Harris County, Texas, also known as METRO, has bus service to town from Terminal C's south side. The airport is served by the 102 Bush IAH Express.

Hotels in and around Houston operate courtesy vans from the airport. There are courtesy phones in baggage claim areas that connect to hotels which offer courtesy vans.

Shuttle service from the airport from various carriers is available to downtown and business district hotels and event venues. Super Shuttle utilizes shared vans to take fliers to communities surrounding the Houston area.

Houston Rental Cars

When you arrive at George Bush Intercontinental Airport, the Consolidated Rental Car Facility, known as CONRAC, takes you to the rental car area. The companies offering rental cars at this airport include Zipcar, Payless, National, Thrifty, E-Z Rent-a-Car, Budget, Enterprise, Dollar, Avis, Alamo and Advantage.

Houston Cabs

You can hail a taxi from a Ground Transportation employee outside each airport terminal. Fare is a flat zone rate to any destination in the Houston city limits.

Payment and Tipping for Taxi's

City of Houston taxi fares are:

$2.75 from meter drop for the first 1/11 mile

$0.20 for each additional 1/11 mile

$2.20 rate per mile after the first mile

$24.00 wait time each hour (calculated at $0.40 per minute)

$1.00 for a late-night surcharge for trips that originate between 8 PM – 6 AM

$2.75 flat Airport departure fee for trips from Bush Intercontinental Airport

Seniors over 60 years old get a 10% discount. Trips to the airport are determined by the zone rates. If your hotel location dictates the use of a toll road, you are responsible for fees. There is not any additional charge for baggage or extra passengers.

You can use credit cards in Houston cabs. And don't forget to tip your taxi cab driver. The recommendation is 10 to 15 percent of the fare.

Uber

You can call for Uber pickups at the airport, or anywhere else in Houston. Learn more and download the app at uber.com.

Public Transport in Houston

METRORail offers accessible, convenient rail service in the downtown area of Houston. Many entertainment, shopping and educational venues are available on the METRORail line.

METRO also offers convenient bus service within the greater Houston area. Local service does run on the main city streets, and stops at every second corner along the route (so it's not a quick trip). One-way fare on a METROBus is $1.25.

Passes & Tickets

Single rides on METRO's Rail or Bus lines are $1.25. A day pass is $3.00, and this will allow you to take advantage of transfers, too. You can purchase passes at the METRO headquarters in downtown Houston, or at retailers found throughout the city.

3. Accommodations

Houston offers a huge variety of options in comfortable accommodations. From living in the lap of luxury to just getting a bed to fall into at the end of the days spent in the busy city, there is something for everyone.

Prices for Luxury Hotels: $320 to $430 per night and up

Four Seasons Hotel Houston
- Close to downtown Houston, Downtown Aquarium, Minute Maid Park, Toyota Center, Discovery Green

The St. Regis Houston
- Close to Williams Tower, Uptown Park, Highland Village, Memorial Park, The Galleria

JW Marriott Houston Downtown
- Downtown Houston, Downtown Aquarium, Discovery Green, Minute Maid Park, Toyota Center

Hotel Sorella City Center
- Close to Memorial Park, Memorial City Mall, Lakeside Country Club, Town and Country Village

The Houstonian Hotel. Club and Spa
- Close to Uptown Park, Houston Arboretum and Nature Center, The Galleria, Memorial Park

The Westin Galleria
- Close to Uptown Park, Highland Village, Gerald D. Hines Waterwall Park, Williams Tower, The Galleria

Prices for Mid-Range Hotels: $200 to $300 per night and up

Westin Oaks at the Galleria
- Close to Highland Village, Gerald D. Hines Waterwall Park, Williams Tower, Memorial Park, The Galleria

Hyatt Centric the Woodlands
- Close to Memorial Hermann, Hughes Landing, Woodlands Mall, Cynthia Woods Mitchell Pavilion, Market Street, Heart of the Woodlands

The Woodlands Waterway Marriott Hotel & Convention Center
- Close to Hughes Landing, Memorial Hermann, Market Street, Woodlands Mall, Cynthia Woods Mitchell Pavilion

Marriott Marquis Houston
- Close to downtown Houston, Downtown Aquarium, Minute Maid Park, Toyota Center, Discovery Green, George R. Brown Convention Center

Omni Houston Hotel
- Close to Williams Tower, Uptown Park, Houston Arboretum and Nature Center, The Galleria, Memorial Park

Royal Sonesta Houston Galleria
- Close to Uptown Park, Gerald D. Hines Waterwall Park, Williams Tower, memorial Park, The Galleria

Prices for Cheaper Hotels: $150 per night and less

Sheraton Houston Brookhollow Hotel
- Close to The Galleria, Memorial Park, Delmar Stadium, Karback Brewing & Tours

Springhill Suites by Marriott Houston/NASA
- Close to Countryside Park, Johnson Space Center (NASA), Space Center Houston, Challenger 7 Memorial Park, Baybrook Mall

Hampton Inn & Suites – Westchase
- Close to Town and Country Village, The Galleria, Arena Theater, Westwood Golf Club

Hilton Houston Galleria
- Close to Menil Collection, Memorial Park, The Galleria, Arena Theater

Holiday Inn Express & Suites
- Close to Town and Country Village, Lakeside Country Club, Edith L. Moore Nature Sanctuary, TopGolf Houston

TownePlace Suites Houston Northwest
- Close to Longwood Golf Club, Willowbrook Mall, Aerodome, Vintage Park

Airbnb's

For $25 per night, you can rent a cozy room close to The Galleria, Downtown, Midtown, the Museum District and Montrose. It's close to public transportation and many nice restaurants.

A private third-story room in a modern three-story townhouse in Midtown will only cost you $150 per night. It's close to nearly everything, even the major highways. The room has contemporary furnishings and you have full access to the kitchen, living room and dining room.

$250 per night can secure you a private bedroom in the Oak Forest community, which is in the northwest part of Houston. It's close to The Galleria Mall, Memorial Park and Bayou Park. It's also close to popular restaurants and bars.

4. Sightseeing

There is not a shortage of things to do when it comes to visiting Houston. Home to the Space Center, inspiring museums, famous artists and renowned chefs, there is so much to see and do – and eat. Houston also offers plenty of green space, even downtown, if you want to step away from the hustle and bustle of the city.

Space Center Houston
This is one of the most famous sights in Houston. It includes 400 artifacts from space, as well as traveling and permanent exhibits related to the manned space flight program of the United States. It's an engaging experience for children and adults alike.

The Galleria
Over 30 million visitors a year seek out the dynamic shopping venue at The Galleria. Locals and visitors blend in seamlessly while entertaining guests at eateries or spending

some quality shopping time. Choose from 400 stores and restaurants, or spend some time at the ice rink, two swimming pools or the children's play area, if they get tired of shopping before you do.

Gerald D. Hines WaterWall Park
This U-shaped, 64-foot WaterWall is the most photographed site in Houston – and that's saying a lot. It has water rushing down its outside and inside walls. It was built in 1985 and utilizes recycled water. Nearly 200 live oak trees shade the area, playing host to families on picnics and people playing with frisbees.

Downtown Aquarium
This is part a sight to see and part restaurant. It's a multi-functional attraction, with its half-a-million-gallon aquarium, a white tiger exhibit, Shark Voyage and a Ferris wheel. The aquarium rather ironically complements their surf-and-turf restaurant menu. People of all ages like to watch the scuba divers who feed fish in the tank.

The Downtown Tunnels

A maze of tunnels spanning six miles connects many of the buildings in the downtown Houston area. The tunnels are more than simply a way to get from point A to point B. There are dozens of restaurants and shops, and you can even stop for a massage.

5. Eat & Drink

There are chefs in Houston who specialize in nearly any cuisine on which you could wish to dine. The Tex-Mex and barbeque scenes have been steadily redesigning themselves, as well. The side dishes in town are as mouth-watering as their meats.

Fine Dining Restaurants

The Pass – approximately $320 for two

The atmosphere at The Pass is modern, and you can see right into the main kitchen. There is even a secret way into the restaurant. They serve five or eight courses, with petit fours and snack bites in between. Some of their favorites include dried sausage with cucumber pannacotta, curry and green peanuts; and squash with bell peppers, bread & ricotta.

Killen's Steakhouse – approximately $275 for two

The ambience at Killen's is plain, and doesn't show you what you're truly in for. The food and the fellowship is what the experience is all about. The service is exceptional – prompt, competent, attentive and friendly. You may want to try the wet or dry aged beef steak, with sautéed mushrooms, jumbo asparagus and potatoes au gratin.

Eddie V's Prime Seafood – approximately $275 for two

This is a popular restaurant, with a nice atmosphere and layout, and a wait staff that will be beside you when you need them, and not otherwise. Among the favorites of the house are Hawaiian yellowtail sashimi with ponzu, cilantro and red chilis, and swordfish steak, broiled with fresh crab, red chilis and avocados.

Oxheart – approximately $245 for two

The service and food at Oxheart are impeccable. Savor each course and the original and inventive flavors. The Spring menu includes "Purple Cosmic" carrots, cooked with onion bouillon; mesquite-smoked swordfish with pickles, mustards, collars and cane syrup; and sausage of grass-fed beef and roast sirloin with dried offal sauce, black tea, citrus leaf and picked beets.

Mid-Range Restaurants

The Capital Grille - approximately $200 for two

The repeat diners here give this restaurant five stars. The music and temperature are just perfect for your eating pleasure. Your server will be ready at a moment's notice, for whatever you need. Among their most enjoyed dishes are sautéed spinach, lobster mac and cheese, crab cakes, lamb chops, salmon and Chilean sea bass.

Quattro – approximately $160 for two

Quattro boasts a lovely atmosphere, an impressive wine selection, and service that is attentive without being imposing. The food is divine, with portion sizes that make you feel like you're getting something besides creativity for your money.

You might like to try the 35-days aged prime ribeye with Tuscan spices, and garlic confit and coco bean. Or perhaps the breaded veal Milanese will tempt your taste buds, served with heirloom tomato and an arugula salad.

Spindletop – approximately $100 for two

You'll find Spindletop in a high downtown Houston tower. There is glass all around and the restaurant turns very slowly, so you can view the whole city. The wait staff are always attentive to your every need. Among the famous dinners are their signature seafood pot for one, with lobster tail, crab claws, fish, smoked sausage, clams, mussels, Gulf shrimp and potato, all in a tasty Ancho chili wine broth. Another favorite is their herb-roasted rack of lamb, with seasonal summer vegetables, mint scented jam, smoked tomato and mesquite scented fingerling potatoes.

<u>Cheap Eats</u> 3-4 listed and described with prices

Barnaby's Café – approximately $30 for two
Barnaby's has a friendly, casual atmosphere with a great wait staff. They are even a dog-friendly restaurant – you probably won't be traveling with your dog, but you should be aware that locals may bring their dogs in. Some of their specialties include Chinese chicken salad, Danish baby back ribs and smoked chicken tostadas.

Teotihuacan Mexican Café – approximately $30 for two
This is a popular Mexican and Tex-Mex restaurant. They have an extensive menu, good prices and huge portions. You might like to try their El Escribano, a beef skirt steak that's topped with Monterey cheese, shrimp scallops

and fresh garlic. Or perhaps you're more in the mood for the Caliente shrimp, which includes five jumbo shrimp in bacon, sautéed with chipotle sauce, bell peppers, jalapenos, onions, tomatoes, wine and fresh garlic.

Sweet Paris Crêperie & Café – approximately $26 for two

This sweet Paris café is found in the Rice Village area. The crepes are delectable and filling. Diners love the chicken carbonara crepes, as well as those made with Nutella and bananas, and their Dulce de leche crepes with berries and coconut flakes.

Fat Bao – approximately $20 for two

This restaurant specializes in Chinese and Fusion cuisine. Don't let the low prices fool you – this is a very popular place. Their fat fries are out of this world. They're hand-cut and then topped with sriracha, onions and cilantro. The Bulgogo Bao is also a favorite, and if you still have room, try a Smores Bao, for something sweet.

6. Culture and Entertainment

Houston is one of the most multicultural cities in the United States, which is itself often referred to as the "Melting Pot". Their international community represents more than 85 nations. Also known as "Bayou City", Houston has neighborhoods that include many Chinese and Vietnamese citizens. The city even has two distinct Chinatowns, one in the downtown area and one on the city's southwest side. It is also home to a Little Saigon, located in Midtown.

Houston Museum District

The Museum District holds 19 community organizations, cultural centers, galleries and museums. They are dedicated to the promotion of culture, history, science and art. They host more than eight million visitors each year. 11 of these museums are always free, while others offer free days or times. The Museum District is bike-able and walkable, with well-maintained, wide sidewalks. The attractions are close to restaurants, so you can take a break when you want to.

Holocaust Museum Houston
This museum is the fourth largest of its kind in the U.S., marking the somber memory of the Holocaust in Europe. Its mission is making more people aware of the dangers that are brought about by violence, prejudice and hatred. The museum strives to promote education, understanding and remembrance, with the goal of tourists, residents and students staying aware or becoming aware of the lessons learned from this tragic event.

Christ Church Cathedral
This is the seat of the Episcopal Diocese in Texas. It was founded in 1839, and has the oldest extant congregation you'll find in Houston. The current building was completed in 1893 and suffered a fire in 1938. It was rebuilt, and became the seat of the Texas diocese in 1949.

Houston Zoo

55 acres of animal wonder are found in the Houston Zoo, located in Hermann Park. They house more than 6,000 animals of 900+ species. They welcome more than two and a half million visitors a year. The zoo offers a unique, fun and inspirational experience, to help people learn to care more about our natural world.

Wet 'n Wild Splash Town

This is a huge water park just north of Houston. Some of its most popular water rides include the six-lane Stingray racer, the wild RipQurl, the Tornado, which uses a tube with four people in it, and Thunder Run. It's a great way to beat that Texas heat in the summer months.

Houston Night-Life

There are no dull moments in Houston's nightlife. The city offers Texas honky-tonks, wine bars and high-energy dance clubs. There is something for everyone. The most explored nightlife districts include Rice Village, Washington Avenue, Montrose, Midtown and Downtown.

Sambuca

This club offers live music every night and delicious, healthy foods on its menu. Their sleek atmosphere and friendly staff keep people coming back for more. It's located in the Rice Hotel, which is a historic place in its own right. Sambuca has an elegant yet simple atmosphere, classic cocktails, an eclectic menu and great entertainment.

Anderson Fair

This venue has welcomed singers like Jewel, and others who are famous now. Some of them still return to flesh out their newest tunes and to share their music with long-time fans. Anderson Fair is among the oldest original and folk music venues in the U.S. It has found its home in Houston since the 1960s.

A different set is offered each night, so the club sees a lot of repeat business. It started out as a coffee house and is now a heavy-hitting club, which offers rookie and seasoned musicians alike a great place to perform.

South Beach

It's a lot shorter drive to the South Beach club in Houston than the flight from Houston to the real South Beach in Florida. The club is found in Montrose, and is a gay-friendly club with an impressive sound system and laser lights. They have liquid ice jets that they shoot over the crowd, and they can really cool off the humid Houston evenings.

7. Special Events in Houston

Martin Luther King Jr. Parade
January
This historic parade celebrates the civil rights leader, marching through the downtown area in Houson. It draws over 300,000 people from all around the nation and the world each January.

Chevron Houston Marathon January
This is an annual event, with a marathon, a half marathon and a three mile run. It winds up at the George Brown Convention Center in the downtown area. It has grown steadily, and now attracts over 20,000 entrants and 200,000 spectators yearly, from all over the world.

Mardi Gras Houston   February
Come on down and celebrate tradition, Creole food and music at the Houston Mardi Gras Parade and festival. The events are filled with fun for the family, dedicated to raising money for vital community needs and to promoting the

Creole culture. Grab a Creole or Southern meal, with crawfish etouffee, gumbo and boudin.

Houston Livestock Show and Rodeo™
March

Houston has held this rodeo as a tradition since 1932. The BRG Park event lasts for three weeks and consumes the city each spring. The Rodeo Parade kicks off the rodeo, and all 20 rodeo competitions finish off with music stars and entertainment.

Bayou City Art Festival Memorial Park
March

This Memorial Park-based festival kicks winter out the door as the premier outdoor fine art event in Houston. Over 300 artists from across the nation work in 19 different media, show their work, are judged and sell some original pieces of art at this festival each year.

Houston Children's Festival   April

The official family celebration of Houston is held each year in the downtowna area. It benefits Child Advicates, Inc. They offer many exciting activities, including 10 family adventure areas, entertainment stages and over 350 games.

WorldFest: Houston International Film Festival   April

WorldFest blends documentaries, music videos, TV commercials, screenplays, short films and feature films for viewers in the area. The fectival has been run since 1968, and past winners are bright stars in entertainment, including George Lucas, Oliver Stone and Steven Spielberg. They won the festival when they were younger, and not as well-known as they are now.

Houston Dragon Boat Festival   May

The Dragon Boat Festival showcases 30 teams that compete on the Buffalo Bayou banks, at Allen's Landing. You can also enjoy Asian cuisine, cultural performances, arts and crafts and music for young and old alike.

Japan Festival — May

Held each year in the Japanese Garden at Hermann Park, the Japan Festival draws over 20,000 people. It celebrates Japan's cultural heritage with two stages, offering bonsai, origami, folk and traditional dance and music.

Free Press Summer Fest — June

This is the largest music festival in Houston, kicking off each summer with big names in music. It takes place on the Buffalo Bayou banks at Eleanor Tinsley Park.

Carnival Houston Show & Parade — June

This event celebrates Carnivale from the New Orleans, Caribbean and Brazlian Mardis Gras. The exciting event features cuisine, music, revelry, and parade and costume performances.

Freedom Over Texas Festival — July

The town's official 4th of July celebration can be found in Eleanor Tinsley Park. It offers food booths, live entertainment and a fireworks display that is world-famous. Celebrate the Independence of the US in the big state of Texas.

Houston International Jazz Festival
August
Downtown Houston plays host to some big names in international jazz. Enjoy some of the summer's hottest music!

Fiestas Patrias   September
Among the most colorful and largest of Southwest community-sponsored parades is held to celebrate the independence of Mexico from Spain. Dancers clad in colorful costumes from local ballet folklorico troupes will spin through the local streets, as they perform to Mexican music.

Oktoberfest Houston   September
Yes, Oktoberfest is in September in Houston – it's on the 30th, though, so it's almost October. This Beer fest has a German twist, and showcases the best of Texas and German culture

on the same day. Enjoy the music, craft beer, and food, too.

Texas Renaissance Festival   October
This festival begins in October and runs for eight weekends, each with a different theme, in Plantersville. It recreates a typical English village from the 16th century. Enjoy comedians, troubadors, minstrels, jugglers and magicians, and period-inspired food and snacks, of course.

Bayou City Art Festival Downtown October
This art show is held annually in Tranquility Park and Hermann Square. It spans several city blocks and holds painting, jewelry and sculptures, along with a kids' zone, beer taverns, wine cafes and great food.

Day of the Dead   November
Dia de los Muertos is a local, traitional holiday to honor and celebrate the lives of friends and family members who have died. It includes arts

and crafts, along with traditional celebrations. The festivities are hosted by the National Museum of Funeral History.

Houston Salutes American Heroes Veterans Day Celebration   November

The city, her people and her mayor show their support for the Armed Forces of the United States each Veterans Day. The annual celebration and parade are a chance for all to show that they stand behind the U.S. Armed Forces.

The Thanksgiving Day Parade
November

This parade is a 60+ year tradition that showcases the Houston community, while entertaining over 200,000 onlookers who line the streets on the morning of Thanksgiving. The impressive parade includes live entertainment, artistic entries, marching bands, flying balloons and the ever-popular floats.

Festival of Lights   November

The holiday magic always glistens a little early at the Festival of Lights in Moody Gardens. There are dozens of scenes and over one million lights. It's such a winter wonderland, with an outdoor ice rink, a gingerbread house, photos with Santa and lots of holiday shopping oppotunities.

Christmas Village at Bayou Bend December

Santa and his stable of reindeer spend time visiting Bayou Bend for 12 fun evenings in December, just in time for the beginning of the holidays. During the Christmas Village event at Bayou Bend, you'll enjoy musical performances, animated projections, sparkling lights and merry decorations.

At the conclusion of the Christmas Village is decorative Spiegeltent – this is a Belgian "tent of mirrors" that has more than 1200 pieces.

8. Safety in Houston

Houston is a busy, big city, so it has petty crime, like most other large cities. If you take precautions and use your common sense, you shouldn't have any problems. Keep your belongings close to you and don't flash valuables or cash around when you're out in public.

The police handle the major tourist areas well, but since there are so many people in these areas, they are still targets for petty crime. Stay away from unfamiliar districts and poorly lit areas at night.

Violent crime is not very common in the tourist areas of Houston. People may attempt to take property or money, but there is generally no force, or even a threat of force, against victims. Carry a street map with you, in case you become lost. Always have a cell phone with you, so that you can contact your hotel for directions, if you need them.

ATM Cautions

Be careful using outdoor ATMs. People could try to stand close enough to you to get your PIN (personal id number), and take your card for their own use.

Conclusion

There is simply no place like Houston. With more than two million residents, the city is attracting award winning cuisine, pro sports, booming business and world-class arts.

Houston is only now enjoying the recognition its locals have felt it has deserved all along. It was named on the Travel & Leisure Roundup of America's Favorite Cities. It was also one of the most affordable US travel destinations, according to Hotwire.com.

We've given you helpful information for every step of your vacation, from planning and booking a hotel to the best places to eat once you're in town. We showed you some of the premier sights and events, too.

See Houston for yourself, where so much happens outdoors, because of mild year-round temps. Explore the culture-filled, eclectic neighborhoods and the Space Center, which is sure to fill you with awe. Enjoy the diverse flavors available in the many restaurants and eateries of Houston.

Printed in Great Britain
by Amazon